The Outdoor Classroom

A place to learn

Hilary Harriman

corner to Learn

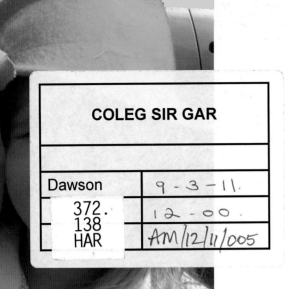

" To my mother, Gwen,
for a lifetime's inspiration."

The Outdoor Classroom

Published by
Corner to Learn Limited
Willow Cottage, 26 Purton Stoke
Swindon, Wiltshire SN5 4JF, UK

www.cornertolearn.co.uk

ISBN: 978-1-905434-07-7

Text © Hilary Harriman 2006

First edition 2006
Reprinted 2010

Series Editor
Neil Griffiths

Editors
Helen O'Neill, Francesca Pinagli

Design
David Rose

Printed in China by
Printworks International Ltd.

Contents

" Children love being out of doors, but if we are going to create a learning environment, then we need to support children to open their eyes to the beauty and excitement which is all around them. Watch together the wonder of leaves fall in Autumn and see new buds appear from seemingly dead branches in Spring. Young children need to see adults being fascinated by nature, excited at finding a spider's web dripping with raindrops, but they also need to learn to value the skill of the spider. To extend that learning, they need the adult to be with them, to model and support them, to read about spiders, draw spiders, be spiders. Learning in the outdoor classroom is not about moving what you have inside, outside. It is using nature as a rich resource to stimulate children's sense of adventure, to build their skills, to open children's eyes and ears to the wonder of what is all around them. To do this, you need to love being outdoors with them. "

Sheila Meadows - Head Teacher,
Caia Park Nursery School, Wrexham

Introduction

The benefits to young children of outdoor play have long been established and acknowledged. It is surprising, therefore, that the outdoor learning environment is still frequently either under-used or used predominantly to promote physical development. This book aims to help teachers and practitioners to re-focus on the outdoor environment and the teaching and learning possibilities that it offers.

In many cases, the outdoor environment is far more practical and more effective for some learning experiences than the indoor environment. When observing young children learn, it is clear that outdoor play opportunities need to be provided alongside indoor play opportunities in order to form a complementary teaching and learning experience.

It is also the case, in a society where technology, in the form of television, videos and computer games, has a high profile with young children, that less time is spent outdoors. Parents are also wary of letting children stray too far from the home. This all leads to a more sedentary, indoor existence for many children. Educational settings need to offer some compensation for this.

Early education practitioners are well versed in organising the indoor teaching space and creating a stimulating and responsive environment in which young children can learn, develop and flourish. The same organisational skills can be utilised to create an outdoor teaching and learning environment that is equally stimulating and responsive.

Practitioners first need to consider what experiences children need to have, and what skills, attitudes and concepts need to be developed. Next, they need to utilise the area or space available appropriately. This applies equally to indoor and outdoor spaces. We should not fall into the trap of allowing the area or space to totally dictate what the learning should be.

The environment itself will stimulate spontaneous play, but the key to creating the most appropriate environment in which young children can explore and develop is **balance**. A sensitive balance between child-initiated and adult-framed play is vital in order for true learning and understanding to take place. There must therefore be careful consideration of what the outdoor space can offer us as a teaching and learning tool, and what the adult can create within that space to stimulate and enhance learning.

To fully utilise an environment that offers, for example, trees, bushes, large areas of grass, small woodland, garden, insect and animal habitats, to which some settings are lucky enough to have access, following the ethos of a **Forest School** would be extremely beneficial (see Chapter 8, *Case studies*).

For many settings, the available outdoor environment can initially seem quite limited. However, with a little imagination, effort and flair, any outdoor space, however limiting it may seem, can become a 'wonderland' for young children to explore and experience with all of their senses.

In the following chapters, we will look at the most commonly discussed barriers to utilising the outdoor environment to its fullest extent. Consideration will also be given to how practitioners can create **Starting points** to stimulate play and effective learning, and meet the requirements of the **early education areas of learning**.

At this point, it is necessary to make a distinction between structured outdoor play and 'playtime'. Structured outdoor play is well planned, purposeful and aimed at giving children valuable and high-quality learning experiences that will help them to develop in all areas of learning. It is very different to a 'break time', where the main purpose is to give children a break from the classroom environment. Structured outdoor play opportunities need to be available throughout the day and will take place in the 'outdoor classroom', just as they do in the indoor classroom.

So, what are the main considerations for organising and managing this outdoor classroom? They mainly fall into the following categories:

- access to and from the area
- size
- design and focus
- Surfaces
- equipment and resources
- health and safety
- storage
- weather
- creating the learning environment, which will be dealt with by focusing on the different areas of learning and offering suggestions for experiences that will enhance children's learning
- the role of the adult

Organisational considerations
Access to and from the area

- Ideally, there should be access from the classroom or inside area to allow for free-flow between the inside and outside areas.
- If the access is not directly from the inside area:
  - how can this be overcome?
  - what are the alternatives?
- Is the area safe and secure?
- Where is the area accessed from? Consider all points of access and ensure that there is safety and security for the children.
- How can this area be staffed in order for good quality teaching and learning to occur?

The answers to these questions will be different for many settings, but should not form a barrier to outdoor learning taking place.

The size of the area

All sizes can be considered as having their own difficulties.

- Small areas can impact on children's behaviour and make activities requiring larger movements difficult to organise.
- Large areas can impact on children's concentration, causing 'flitting' between activities; some children can be overwhelmed by large spaces, and staff can tend to become supervisors rather than learning enhancers.

Making the best of the space available – some considerations

If the space is small:

- combine the indoor and outdoor space and create one whole environment, i.e. some activities happen inside, some outside, and the children rotate or 'flow'.
- prioritise activities or change them to provide a balance over time.
- prioritise the use of equipment so that this provides a balance over time.

If the space is large (e.g. schoolyard):

- think about dividing the area into designated areas of learning.
- create bays with their own specific focus.
- create smaller areas with false barriers.

The design and focus

- Just as a classroom is not left as an empty open space, designate the outdoor space in a similar way to the classroom.
- Develop the outdoor space into a stimulating teaching and learning environment.
- Consider which activities work best next to each other, where the walkways between should be, and how inviting the area is for children.
- Research has shown that outdoor areas can be over-designed and the space too controlled, leaving the children with no opportunity to affect the space.
- A **free** space (i.e. no fixed equipment) where staff can create the learning areas they wish is often a more effective learning space.

Suggested areas

- Children's play should use the equipment, not be dictated by it.
- Consider the equipment and the resources best suited to the planned learning experiences, not just best suited to outdoors.
- Seating outdoors is essential. Have a good variety, be imaginative and do not restrict it to being fixed.

Imaginative · Investigation · Gardening · Building and construction · Physical ← **Outdoor play** → Creative · Experimental · Quiet area · Scientific discovery · Large and small motor skills

Surfaces

- Hard surfaces and soft surfaces (in the form of rubber or grass) can offer different opportunities for the types of equipment and activities for which you can cater.
- If there are no soft surfaces, create them with carpet squares or similar material.
- If you have no 'garden' area, create one with raised beds, tubs, containers, etc.
- If there is too much grass, which is difficult to use when wet, consider changing it, making it smaller, providing suitable footwear, or creating pathways with alternative surface materials.
- Try not to let the surface stop you from being imaginative about how to use the space.

Equipment and resources

- How necessary is fixed equipment? Some research indicates that areas with the most fixed equipment often have a lower rating of play.
- Research has also shown that often areas with the highest ratings of play had equipment which could be manoeuvred by the children.
- For the remaining bulkier equipment (if there is no designated outdoor equipment store), either invest in a storage shed or store equipment near to the access door.
- Alternate the equipment so that the heavier items are not always in use.
- Plan the **learning experience** first, then provide the appropriate equipment.

Health and safety

The issue of safety in the outdoor environment needs to be considered very carefully. Although the same health and safety concerns that are prevalent in the indoor classroom will also apply to the outdoor classroom, there are some issues that are very specific to the outdoors.

> " We must not let our aversion to risk reduce opportunities for young people to appreciate the awe and wonder of nature ... "
>
> *Hywyn Williams, Chief Officer for Learning and Achievement, Wrexham*

Key questions are:

- Does the area have a secure boundary?
- Are the surfaces appropriate for the activities that will take place upon them, e.g. a soft rubberised surface under climbing equipment?
- Is the equipment checked regularly for any danger points, breakages, weaknesses, splinters, etc.?
- Are the resources in use safe to handle, appropriate to the tasks and well maintained?
- Are all the children and adults aware of, and regularly reminded about, the rules for safe behaviour in the outdoor environment?
- Is any metal equipment checked before use? Metal can become: dangerous if hot to the touch in sunny weather and may need covering up before use; slippery in wet weather and will need to be wiped before use.

- Has the area been carefully checked for bottles, glass, syringes, etc., daily, before the children use it? (Remember to wear protective clothing when collecting any dangerous items.)
- Has the area been checked daily for signs of animal use? (Always use lids to cover sandpits, water, etc.)
- Has the setting informed parents of the need for safe and appropriate footwear and clothing for the outdoor environment?
- Has the positioning of equipment been duly considered, e.g. the danger of having wheeled vehicles under climbing frames?
- Are all types of weather catered for, including the need for shade from strong sunlight, e.g. tents, parasols, teepees, arbours, pergolas, trees, etc.?
- Does a regular risk-assessment take place, focusing on the safety of the space and materials?

Storage

This is the most common area of concern among practitioners.

- The first consideration must be the equipment and resources. Consider which is most effective and most frequently used; re-consider anything too bulky or not versatile enough and dispense with anything that is not really needed.
- Try not to think of outdoor play only in terms of physical development – rather think in terms of **all-round** development, where much of the equipment needed may be small and lightweight.

Weather

- Weather has to be 'worked with' in order for children not to miss out.
- All weather conditions need to be considered, including shade and protection from the sun.
- If a veranda or similar shaded area is not available, create a pergola or covered archway.
- Trees can provide shade from the sun, as can an open-sided tent construction, pergolas, pop-up tents, awnings, covered archways.
- In colder weather, ensure that there are spare gloves, scarves, coats, etc. for those who need extra clothing.
- Try not to let the weather constantly dictate how the outdoor environment is used. Most weather conditions can be dealt with by providing appropriate clothing.

1 Personal, social, emotional development

Common teaching and learning elements

- Building self-confidence
- Forming positive relationships
- Developing independence
- Gaining an awareness of the children's own emotional and physical needs and those of others
- Demonstrating appropriate expression of feelings and understanding of the needs of others
- Understanding and acceptance of other cultures and beliefs
- Developing a positive attitude to learning
- Learning to co-operate with, and relate to, others
- Caring for the environment and living things

Outdoor classroom opportunities

Outdoor circle-time

Use circle-time / get-together-time to concentrate on the following:

- Appropriate outdoor play behaviour
- Health and safety issues relating to the outdoor environment
- Caring for the outdoor environment and the living creatures and plants within it
- Encouraging independence in the use of outdoor equipment, materials, resources and how and where to find and store them
- Building confidence in the children's ability to use, explore and manipulate the outdoor environment
- Recognising the needs of others and demonstrating appropriate expression of feelings
- Introducing routines and rules for using the outdoor environment
- Stories, games, songs and rhymes relating to the outdoor environment
- Larger scale, more physical circle-time games
- Large, co-operative circle games such as **The Farmer's in His Den**

Outdoor role-play

Utilise the outdoor environment to create role-play areas that relate to outdoor activities, e.g:

Street Market **Journeys** **Holidays**

Street Café **Camping** **Summer Fête**

Garden Centre **Another Planet**

The Zoo **Sea / Pirate Adventure**

The Fairground **Fairytales**

Garage **Teddy Bears' Picnic**

The Wild Wood **Primordial Swamp**

Builder's Yard and Building Site

The Emergency (e.g. car accident, fire
See Chapter 8, *Case studies*)

(Focus on the Personal, Social and Environmental elements within each theme.)

Sharing games

- Act out stories with a sharing theme, e.g. **The Little Red Hen**.
- Use team games focusing on teamwork and co-operative working, e.g. group **Obstacle Course**, team races, treasure hunts, etc.
- Use large circle **Pass the Parcel** (or ball or toy type of game) that encourages co-operation and turn-taking. Include fun forfeits to enhance the game's possibilities.
- Use **Open the Box**, a group game involving:
  - taking turns to guess what is in the box
  - rules and instructions for opening the box
  - solutions for unwrapping the box
  - a participating task for each child within the box
  - something in the box that can be shared equally

Create a carnival

- The children work in groups to create stalls, games, side-shows, etc. in preparation for a class fête or carnival (link into the role-play area and Summer Fête).
- Discuss different carnival traditions, e.g. the Jersey Flower Festival, Mardi Gras, the Notting Hill Carnival, or other traditional British carnivals.

(Alternatively, link this to multi-cultural festivals and act out.)

Suggestions for resources

- flags, balloons, paper streamers, banners
- brightly-coloured material
- dressing-up clothes
- card, glue, paper plates, paint, collage
- items / doweling to make masks
- musical instruments
- tape recorder or CD player
- materials to make own instruments, e.g. shakers, drums
- items for open-air stalls, e.g. cake stall, tombola, throw the hoop over the skittles, coconut shy

Weather games

- Create games that link to different types of weather, i.e. the children work together and with adults to create a 'sunny-day play box', a 'rainy-day play box', a 'windy-day play box', etc. which would contain activities appropriate to the weather. The play boxes would then be available for the children to access the activities on the relevant 'weather day'.

(See Chapter 5 for seasonal activities.)

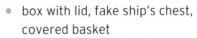

The environmental 'Treasure chest'

- The children create a 'treasure chest' of drawings, pictures, artefacts, etc. relating to their immediate or local environment, focusing on caring for the environment and living things.
- The 'chest' then becomes a focus for a circle-time or get-together-time outdoors to encourage discussion on environmental issues.
- Change the contents of the chest on a regular basis or change the theme, e.g. 'The things I like to do outside', 'Our holiday treasure chest', or 'Our visit treasure chest'.

Suggestions for resources

- box with lid, fake ship's chest, covered basket
- items found in local environment, e.g:
  feathers
  stones
  leaves
  flowers
  twigs
  seed heads
  cones or other seeds from trees
  mini-beasts, e.g. snails, wood-lice, ladybirds, caterpillars

The items will change according to the focus you are creating.

Mini-sports day

- The children help to develop and create races and events that will be part of a mini-sports day or session, linking Personal, Social and Emotional Development with Physical Development.
- The children will test their events and practise for each event in the lead-up to the mini-sports day session, which will focus on teamwork, supporting each other and celebrating success.

Super-heroes

- This activity is based on popular comic-strip characters such as **Spiderman** and **Wonder Woman**, and creates new super-heroes for the children to role-play.
- Focus on the need for super-heroes to help others and to come to their aid when they are in need.
- Create super-hero costumes, which can include practising dressing and fastening skills at the same time.
- Create super-hero characteristics for each role, e.g. 'Environment Man' and 'Tree Girl', and devise situations and services for the super-hero to act out.

Celebrate the seasons

- Link each season to a series of activities focusing on weather cycles, seasonal cycles, seasonal traditions and activities, festivals and changes in the environment.
- Create a seasonal-related activity box for outdoor play containing activities relating to different times of the year, e.g. snow activities, springtime activities, Easter egg hunt, Maypole dancing, harvest time, etc.

  (For a list of seasonal activities, see Chapter 5, *Knowledge and understanding of the world*.)
- For this section on Personal, Social and Emotional Development, keep the focus of the seasonal activities upon the awe and wonder aspect of the changing seasons.
- Use the changing of the seasons to focus also on a wide range of multi-cultural religious festivals and traditions associated with each season, e.g. Easter, Whitsun, Christmas, Ramadan, Divali, Eid and Rosh Hashanah.

Fun with sand and water

- Take sand and water activities into the outdoor environment, but make them on a larger scale, e.g. create a 'beach' area with enough sand for the children to take off their shoes and socks and get into. Similarly, invest in a large inflatable paddling pool for larger water activities.

(Always ensure children are fully supervised during such activities.)

Garden party

- Spend time with the children preparing for a garden party. Discuss different types of party and celebrations. Link into different cultures and traditions.
- Create numerous activities leading up to the party, e.g:
  - preparing food / creating a refreshment tent
  - decorating the outdoor party space
  - making and sending invitations
  - creating party games
  - dressing-up
- Have the party – have fun!

Suggestions for resources

- a tent or material to make a marquee
- various ingredients for preparing food, e.g. sandwiches, cakes, strawberries and cream, etc.
- flags, balloons, bunting, streamers, banners
- materials to make party invitations
- dressing-up clothes
- items relating to party games, e.g. **Pass the Parcel**, **Musical Chairs**
- seating and tables for refreshments
- stalls and side-shows, e.g. puppet theatre, bandstand, fish for a duck: make fishing rods with hooks and fasten fabric rings to numbered plastic ducks

Going on a journey

- Focusing on different modes of transport, help the children to create buses, trains, aeroplanes and boats from construction equipment, cardboard boxes, wheeled vehicles, etc.
- Focus on a different form of transport each session, i.e. vehicles that travel: on roads, in the air, on the sea, on rails.
- Discuss destinations, other countries, how to get there.
- Go on an imaginary 'journey', make a map, talk about what you saw, etc.

Suggestions for resources

- construction material and equipment for the children to construct different types of vehicle
- small-world equipment
- toy vehicles
- books and maps describing various destinations
- IT for information on other countries
- paper, card, pencils, etc. to make maps of an imaginary journey

2 Language, literacy and communication skills

Common teaching and learning elements

Speaking and Listening

- Communicating and interacting with others
- Using speech to organise, sequence and clarify thoughts, feelings and events
- Understanding the codes of conduct related to speaking and listening, e.g. taking turns
- Using language to express imagination or retell stories or experiences
- Being an effective listener
- Listening with enjoyment
- Listening with understanding
- Exploring and creating sounds, words, stories, rhymes, etc.

Reading and Writing

- Knowing that print carries meaning
- Knowing the conventions of reading in English, e.g. left to right, top to bottom, etc.
- Hearing and saying 'sounds'
- Linking sounds to letters and naming and sounding the letters of the alphabet
- Beginning to recognise familiar words and simple sentences
- Beginning to show an understanding of the main elements of a story
- Using their understanding of sounds to form words
- Beginning to make marks to represent writing
- Beginning to recognise and use a variety of written forms
- Refining fine motor skills to enable a comfortable grip of writing implements
- Beginning to form recognisable letters with growing control over formation

Outdoor classroom opportunities
Environmental print

Starting points

- Spend time with the children making labels for the environmental items which can be found in their outdoor classroom. Include resources and equipment.
- Discuss the sounds that make up each word.
- Create games where the children have to find and match words to objects, e.g:
  1 Hide different items in the outdoor environment, e.g. a picture, a teddy, a toy, a small treasure box.
  2 Show the children a picture of an item, or name it, then show the label.
  3 The children then have to find the item, return to the 'label centre' and match the correct label to the item.

(This could also be played as an 'initial sound' game.)

- Create games that focus on initial sounds and final sounds, i.e. a 'run and touch' I spy game.
- Encourage the children to create their own outdoor classroom labels using drawings and developmental writing.
- As a group, read the labels regularly to familiarise the children with the sound and sight of the words.
- Hide secret messages around the outdoor environment, e.g:
  - hanging from a tree
  - buried in the sand tray or pit
  - in a bottle in a water tray

Give the children word clues as to where the secret message might be (in the form of a word map).

Example:

Start → Garden bench → Tree → Water tray → Sand tray → Secret message

Re-create a story

- Using role-play, encourage the children to retell favourite stories, nursery rhymes, etc. by acting them out in the outdoor environment.
- Encourage the children to sequence the story and talk about or demonstrate 'what happened next'.
- In the outdoor space, create the appropriate environment for a story, e.g. stories that take place in a wood, in a castle, in the sea, in a garden, etc.
- Explore frightening or 'scary' environments so that the children can come to terms with their fears.
- Put on an impromptu outdoor 'performance' of a play or story by 'directing' the children through events.

Somewhere to write

- Do not forget to offer the children an opportunity to write in the outdoor classroom.
- Create a writing place such as a bench, an arbour, a corner or a tent to encourage the children to see writing as an outdoor as well as an indoor activity.

> " Positive experiences both indoors and out which enable children to discover and explore the joy of mark-making are invaluable. "
>
> *Alison Heale – Advisory Teacher*

Role-play

- Utilise the ideas for outdoor role-play from the Personal, Social and Emotional Development (PSE) section in Chapter 1, to encourage speaking, listening, reading and writing skills.

It's a small world!

- Utilise small-world toys and equipment to create opportunities for language skills to develop, i.e. create small-world play situations, e.g:
  - the farm
  - at the garage
  - the train journey
  - the view of a village and landscape from a hot air balloon
  - at the Zoo
  - at the seaside
  - the prehistoric world
- Utilise the situations to promote speaking and listening skills, questioning, reasoning, lines of enquiry, etc.
- Follow up with simple reading and writing skills, e.g. labelling, writing a simple story-line for each situation, making lists, etc.

Large construction

- Use the outdoor space to create larger-scale building opportunities for the children.
- Link these larger-scale building activities to role-play scenarios, e.g:
  - a castle for a fairytale setting
  - cages and pens for animals at the Zoo
  - fairground rides
  - building site construction
- Use large construction equipment to encourage the children to create scenarios for stories and events to be acted out, e.g. as in 'Going on a Journey' role-play in the Personal, Social and Emotional Development (PSE) section in Chapter 1.

Word games and instruction cards

- Create outdoor games related to sounds and words, e.g:
  - letter / sound / word 'hunts'
  - 'related words' game, e.g. *petal, stalk, leaf* all go together because they make up a flower.
- Create instruction games focusing on:
  - action words / verbs
  - prepositions, e.g. Obstacle Course
  - 'Find me a ...' games (nouns)
  - verb + adverb games, e.g. run fast, walk slowly
  - adjective games, e.g. 'Where is the blue ball / spotted dog?' etc.
- Begin with spoken instructions and build up to picture / word cards, then word only, etc.

The imaginary journey

- Having created a role-play bus, train, ship, etc., encourage the children to imagine what they see on a journey to the jungle, the seaside, the shops, etc.
- Gather the children's thoughts together and create the imaginary journey in pictures, words or writing so that it can be read back to them.

Magic writing

- Utilise all available surfaces and tools for writing opportunities, e.g:
  - large letter formation in large sand pit
  - writing in the air
  - writing letters with paint brushes and water on walls, yard, etc.
  - Take painting or writing easels outside and encourage writing with paint, chalk, etc.

Suggestions for resources

- large sand tray or pit
- sticks for making marks
- variety of sizes of paintbrush, buckets or containers for water
- easels, paint, chalk, crayons
- large surfaces for children to make marks, e.g. sheets

The listening walk

- Take groups of children on a 'listening' walk around the outdoor environment. Encourage them to focus on the sounds they hear and keep a tally of them. (This can take many forms. Decide on one with the children.)

- Following the walk, encourage the children to make a record of what they have heard. Make a listening map or graph, or a listening-walk story.

Be a 'People person'

- Look at the roles of people from the children's everyday life, e.g. postman / woman, school crossing patrol, farmer, gardener, bus driver, police or fire department personnel, builder, pilot, train driver, milkman, newspaper deliverer, zoo keeper, photographer.

  (Keep the focus mainly on outdoor jobs to link with the outdoor classroom.)

- Invite people to visit the outdoor classroom and talk about their job and how it relates to the outdoor environment.

- Create scenarios for the children to act out the roles that have been discussed.

3 Mathematical development

Common teaching and learning elements

- Using number songs, rhymes, stories and simple counting games
- Developing the following abilities in a variety of contexts:
    - to classify / sort
    - to match
    - to order
    - to sequence
    - to compare
    - to count
- Beginning to recognise and use numbers
- Matching numbers to sight and sound
- Beginning to understand mathematical concepts such as 'less' and 'more', etc.
- Recognising and making patterns

- Beginning to recognise and name shapes (flat and solid), size and colours
- Demonstrating the practical elements of weighing and measuring
- Beginning to understand the mathematics of money, time and position
- Using mathematical language for:
    - number
    - shape
    - size
    - position
    - measurement, etc.
- Beginning to show an interest in problem-solving and demonstrate methods of finding solutions

Outdoor classroom opportunities
Picnics

- As with other areas of learning, the possibilities for Mathematical Development during role-play are vast. (See the PSE section in Chapter 1 for suggestions, e.g. **Teddy Bears' Picnic**.)
- Plan the picnic focusing on the following:
  - how many will attend
  - invitations
  - timing
  - locations
  - what preparations are needed
  - how many cushions, cups, cakes, etc.
- Prepare the picnic, focusing on buying and measuring ingredients, amounts of items, estimating, etc.
- During the picnic, focus on:
  - counting
  - matching
  - discussing time / sequence of events
  - one to one correspondence
  - sharing out
  - measuring and comparing
  - sorting and tidying up

Suggestions for resources

- card, glue, pens, glitter, etc. to create invitations, or use IT
- ingredients to make food
- paper plates, cups, spoons, bowls, etc.
- rugs, cushions or carpet squares for sitting on
- baskets for picnic
- number / colour cards for matching games
- waste bins for collecting litter

Patterns in the environment / Pattern hunt

- Use the environment to focus on natural and man-made patterns. Have a pattern hunt on, e.g:
  - buildings
  - trees and leaves
  - flowers and leaves
  - insects / birds
  - clouds in the sky
  - fences / gates
  - windows and doors

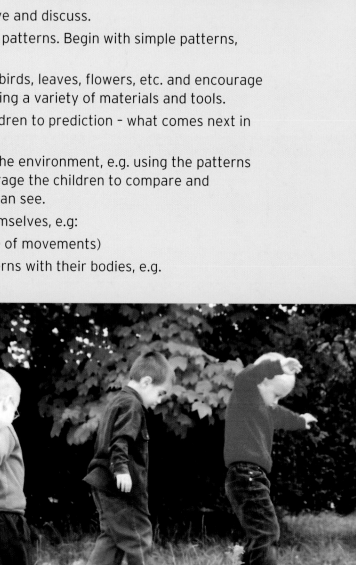

- Use this opportunity to encourage the skills of sorting, comparing, ordering and sequencing.
- Make a collection of outdoor patterns to observe and discuss.
- Encourage the children to create and re-create patterns. Begin with simple patterns, then move to more complex ones.
- Look at patterns in nature, e.g. butterflies, ladybirds, leaves, flowers, etc. and encourage the children to discuss and create their own, using a variety of materials and tools.
- Use patterns around them to introduce the children to prediction - what comes next in a given pattern.
- Focus on size, shape and colour of patterns in the environment, e.g. using the patterns available in the environment (as above), encourage the children to compare and contrast the size, shape and colours that they can see.
- Create physical patterns using the children themselves, e.g:
  - patterns in movement (created as a sequence of movements)
  - group patterns (groups of children form patterns with their bodies, e.g. large circles, small squares, etc.)

Obstacle course

- Create an obstacle course that can feature in a variety of games that consist of following instructions. Focus on the children's listening skills and their understanding of positional language.
- Create sets of instructions that use a range of positional language, e.g:
  - *Crawl **through** the tunnel and jump **up** and **down** until you reach the bench.*
  - *Step **up** onto the bench, walk **forwards** and jump off the end.*

Let's build!

- Use large construction equipment to focus on mathematical elements of shape and size.

- Encourage the correct use of mathematical language related to shape and size.

- Create a builder's yard or building site area and give the children projects to work on. Link this to the role-play themes and encourage the children to create, e.g:

    - a castle for a fairytale theme

    - vehicles for a transport theme

    - stalls, games, etc. for a garden party

- Encourage the children to make simple design plans and think about materials, how they are going to connect or join different pieces, etc. Here there is much scope, not only for mathematical concepts, but also for design and technology skills.

- Build on a grand scale because, outdoors, the children will not be as limited in what they can produce as they would be indoors.

Suggestions for resources

- building blocks – various sizes
- planks / flat construction items
- curved blocks for bridges
- boxes and card
- flexible pipe and guttering
- hoops
- ropes, string, pegs
- old blankets, sheets or large pieces of material
- builder's tray and building material
- shoe boxes, kitchen roll tubes
- pebbles, stones, shells
- twigs, small sticks
- wheelbarrows, trolleys or crates
- workbench and construction tools
- various types of adhesive and fasteners

Number action rhymes and songs

- Outside, this can be done on a larger scale. There are numerous counting songs and rhymes relating to the outdoor environment that would benefit from a larger physical space in which to play them out. Examples are **Five Little Speckled Frogs**, **Five Little Ducks**, **One, Two, Three, Four, Five. Once I Caught a Fish Alive**, **Ten in the Bed**.

- Compile a list of outdoor number rhymes and songs which can be introduced during outdoor play.

- With the children, devise your own number rhymes and songs for use outdoors. Include some with larger numbers.

Washing day

- Create a laundry area with a washing line, washing baskets, an assortment of clothes, pegs, washing bowls, water, washing powder, etc.
- Utilise this area to encourage children to focus on the following as they wash and hang out their washing:
  - capacity
  - sorting
  - matching
  - sequencing
  - colour
  - pattern
  - size
  - shape

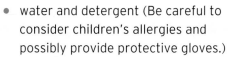

- Use number labels to encourage sequencing of numbers on the line.
- Use the washing line to focus on time, e.g:
  - create time lines for a sequence of pictures, drawings or paintings
  - sequence the children's day, e.g. getting up, coming to school, having a snack, etc.

“ There is a clear emphasis on early education through play and where better to play than outside, and yes in the rain, mud and all that goes with it ... ”

Hywyn Williams, Chief Officer for Learning and Achievement, Wrexham

Treasure hunt

- Utilise the idea of a 'treasure hunt'. Hide objects, or 'treasure', for the children to find in the outdoor area, e.g. shiny objects, toys, play coins, treasure chest.

  or

  Theme the 'treasure', e.g:
  - different types of jewellery
  - various soft toy animals
  - number / shape / colour cards
  - items attached to a well-known story
  - themed story books

- Link the 'treasure' to matching, counting, sorting games, e.g:

  Have five treasure boxes labelled 1 to 5. Give the children a set time to find objects. When time is up, they count how many they have found and put them into the correct treasure box.

- There is a range of games that can be developed, based on the format of the game above, which could focus on:
  - numbers
  - size
  - shape
  - simple addition / subtraction
  - more / less, etc.

Gardening

Create a garden area and utilise it to explore the following mathematical concepts:

- Capacity, e.g. How much soil will these pots hold?
- Use of mathematical language, e.g. *more / less than*, *empty / full*, etc.
- Ordering of size of pots, plants, buckets, etc.
- Estimating, e.g. How many seeds will fill the pot? What size hole will we need to dig?
- Measuring, e.g. width of pots, length of flower beds, growth of plants, etc.

Suggestions for resources

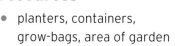

- planters, containers, grow-bags, area of garden
- digging equipment
- rakes and sieves
- plant pots – a variety of sizes
- plants, herbs, seeds
- buckets, bowls and similar containers
- watering cans
- gardening gloves
- measuring equipment: tape measures, measuring sticks, rulers, etc.
- a variety of capacity equipment to measure sand, soil, water, etc.

Crossing the river

1 Create a 'pretend' river with lily pads crossing it, using card or mats to represent the lily pads.
2 The children take turns to throw a dice and move themselves, a frog or a beanbag across the lily pads.
3 Use colours, shapes, numbers on the lily pads with a corresponding dice.
4 Put forfeits on the lily pads to encourage moving on and moving back, counting on and counting back.

Market day

- Develop the role-play theme of a street market to incorporate a range of mathematical skills and concepts.

- Write shopping lists – what? / how many? This can be extended by giving the children a list of different items to be bought in picture or word form, then checking how successfully they have completed their shopping trip.

- Plan the journey to the market. Use positional language.

- Encourage the understanding and use of money, i.e. can the children recognise and read the price of an item, buy an item giving correct money, count how much money they have left, and so on?

Suggestions for resources

- tables to create market stalls
- material to create awnings
- items for stall holders to sell
- writing materials for lists and directions
- shopping bags, handbags, purses
- money
- price lables
- number labels

Car park

1 Paint or chalk large shapes onto the outdoor play surface to form car parking spaces, e.g. square, circle, triangle. Use a selection of wheeled vehicles, numbered and shaped parking tickets and signs for each parking space.

2 Direct the children to a specific number or shape. They then identify it and take the correct parking ticket.

3 Extend the above with counting and estimating activities or instructions to reinforce positional language, e.g. *Put the blue car behind the red truck.*

Tallying games

- These can be any game such as skittles, where the children have to keep a score by using a tally.

Skittles

1 The children take turns to knock down the skittles and record their score in tallies after each throw. They use a mark or symbol for each skittle.

2 On completion of the game, each child counts the sum total of their tallies to discover the final score.

(This can be adapted to tossing balls into a bin, or quoits or beanbags into a hoop, etc.)

How many did you see?

1 The children are given a set time to look for various items, e.g. vehicles, birds, shapes, flowers.

2 Each item seen is given a tally which corresponds to a simple column block graph.

3 When the set time is up, the totals are counted to see which column has the most, the fewest, the same, etc.

> " From seeing the symmetry of leaves and butterfly wings to counting the rings of a trunk to calculate the tree's age ... maths is all around us. "
>
> *Nigel Davies – Maths Teaching and Learning Adviser*

4 Physical development

Common teaching and learning elements

- Moving confidently with control, co-ordination and safety
- Showing an awareness of space in relation to self and others
- Becoming aware of the importance of health and fitness
- Using small and large equipment and developing fine and gross motor skills
- Handling tools and equipment with increasing control
- Enjoying physical activities and using the body for expression of feelings and responses to stimulation of the senses

Outdoor classroom opportunities

Parcel delivery

(Also effective in promoting mathematical skills.)

- Set up an outdoor postal sorting office for wrapping and delivering parcels.

- Provide boxes / items for wrapping, and a variety of materials and equipment with which to wrap them.

- Allow the children to explore the possibilities and properties of the materials in order to make informed choices about how and why to use them.

- Encourage the use of developmental writing for labelling, addressing, etc.

- Focus on fine motor skills and co-ordination during the wrapping process.

- Link this physical development to opportunities for mathematical concept and skill development, e.g. shape, counting, estimating, sorting, matching.

- Use the parcels for guessing games as to what they contain.

- Devise a delivery service using wheeled vehicles and construction equipment.

Health and fitness festival

- Over a period of time, focus on:
  - healthy eating
  - how our bodies work
  - staying fit and healthy

  Emphasise the importance of exercise (particularly outdoors), fresh air and a healthy diet. Use the outdoor classroom to reinforce the positive aspects of being outdoors.

- Devise 'fitness' and 'keeping healthy' sessions with physical activities which focus on a range of recognised fitness-promoting sports. Try simple group versions of team and individual sports, e.g. cricket, tennis, athletics.

- Culminate these activities in a special health and fitness event or festival where all the outdoor activities for that day focus on physical development.

Small equipment-time

- Introduce a variety of small sports equipment such as balls, hoops, ropes, quoits, beanbags, skittles, etc.
- Spend time demonstrating the skills needed to use the sports equipment effectively, e.g. throwing, catching, kicking, aiming. (This can also be utilised to promote directional language.)
- Allow ample time for the children to experiment with the equipment and practise their skills.
- Set 'time trials', e.g. How many times can you throw and catch the ball in three minutes using a sand timer?
- Hold a 'mini-sports gala' to celebrate the children's achievements.

Mirror games

- Concentrate on physical movement and how the body can move in the outdoor space.
- Encourage the children to experiment with different kinds of movement, to move freely and with pleasure and confidence.
- In pairs or in groups with a rotating leader, encourage one child to devise a sequence of movement for their partner or group to 'mirror'.
- Extend the game by giving the leader a characteristic on which to base their movements, e.g. move like a robot, monkey, ballet dancer, bird, etc.

" If it can be done indoors, it can probably be done bigger, better and more meaningfully outdoors! "
Carl Wynn – Link Support Teacher

Build an obstacle course

- Following on from the obstacle course theme in the Mathematical Development section, encourage the children to plan and create their own obstacle course.

- The children will need access to large and small construction equipment, sports equipment, cardboard boxes and large tubes, etc.

- The children will need to think carefully about the body movements necessary to manoeuvre their course. They will also need to consider safety issues.

- Each obstacle will need to be rehearsed and checked for safety and degree of difficulty before other children are allowed to participate.

  (Again, there will be ample opportunity to introduce and reinforce positional and directional language.)

Outdoor statues

- Offer the children a theme on which to base their statue game, e.g.
  - animal statues
  - shape statues
  - vehicle statues, etc.

- Encourage the children to focus on controlling their bodies for lack of movement, i.e. keeping still, for a set period of time, as well as the control they need in order to create movement.

" Seeing my grandson enjoying the outdoors, in a muddy field, on a bitterly cold day, not only gave him a healthy glow, but gave me a glow of satisfaction. "

Rosemary Beynon - Former Nursery Nurse and Grandmother

5 Knowledge and understanding of the world

Common teaching and learning elements

- Beginning to develop the children's understanding of the world around them by using their senses
- Experimenting with a wide variety of materials and learn about their properties
- Beginning to sort things into groups and look at similarities and differences
- Beginning to design and make things, making choices about appropriate resources and materials
- Solving problems by experimenting, asking questions and making decisions
- Beginning to appreciate the importance of the environment and recognise pattern, shape and changes in the world around them
- Learning about ways to care for the environment
- Observing, appreciating and caring for living things, with a sense of respect
- Talking about the seasons and the weather
- Developing an awareness of the children's own bodies, growth, hygiene, diet, exercise and personal safety
- Developing an appreciation of nature and a sense of awe and wonder
- Talking about where the children live
- Beginning to understand different places
- Talking about the world of work
- Talking about, and beginning to understand, the idea of time
- Beginning to learn about past and present events in familiar contexts
- Becoming aware of the use of a variety of information sources

Outdoor classroom opportunities

Treasure baskets / boxes

- The children are asked to collect a variety of 'treasures of nature' within their outdoor environment, e.g. a stone, a leaf, a blade of grass, a snail, a picture of a cloud, using all their senses. They put these carefully into their own individual treasure basket to bring back to a circle-time discussion on what they have found.

- The discussion is the opportunity to discover how much the children already know about nature and living things, and will form the basis for other related activities which aim to extend their knowledge. This opportunity to talk specifically about things they have found and noticed is a vital element of assessing their knowledge and understanding, and should not be rushed.

Suggestions for resources – themed baskets

- touch / feel
- smell
- hear
- shiny objects
- music box
- weighing box
- measuring box
- shape box
- collections box
- colour box
- time basket
- words and sounds basket
- number box
- investigation basket
- tools basket
- threading basket
- construction box
- materials basket

Treasure trails

- Extensions to the above theme could involve setting up a treasure trail with picture, word, sound or touch clues that the children must solve in order to find the 'treasure'.

    In this way, adults can focus the children's attention on using a particular sense, or on a particular kind of 'treasure', e.g. different leaves, groups of similar things, a variety of mini-beasts.

    If the children work to solve the clues in pairs or small groups, you will also be encouraging discussion and communication skills, together with inter-personal skills and co-operation.

Treasure maps

- These activities can encourage an understanding of the environment at the same time as developing the children's positional, geographical and early mapping skills.

  Initially, the adult can create 'treasure maps' for the children to follow around the outdoor environment with 'treasures' hidden to find along the way.

  There will be a wealth of opportunity for the children to develop an understanding of how maps work. When they are familiar with this, they can begin to create their own 'treasure' maps:
  - for an adult to follow
  - for their partners to follow
  - for a group of their peers to follow

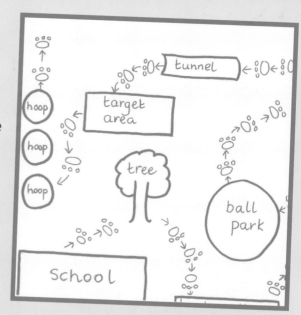

Treasure displays

- Following the discovery of 'treasures', particularly those related to nature and the environment, create treasure displays for these purposes:
  - to initiate discussion
  - to give a focus to particular elements of teaching and learning, e.g. caring for living things
  - for observational drawings, painting and models
  - as a focus for particular language / word / sound skills

Note: Don't forget that displays are equally effective when created outdoors. They need only be on display for short periods of time - long enough to focus the children's attention and concentration.

Create a habitat

- Using sand, water, soil, stones, etc. and small-world play resources, encourage the children to create world-wide habitats in the outdoor environment that reflect what they know about the world and have heard about in stories.

- Initiate this activity by discussions or with a series of stories about people and animals in other parts of the world.

- The children can then discuss and make choices about which habitat to create, e.g. jungle, desert, under the sea, garden, and which resources to use.

- Ensure that there are areas set aside in the outdoor classroom for this work to take place.

- Once the children have created their own habitats, let them all visit each one in turn and ask the creators to talk about their own particular habitat, and what they might expect to find living there.

Environmental 'sound and photo shoot'

- This can take place within the outdoor classroom area - or you may wish to organise a visit or walk to take in a wider area of the environment.

  There could be a general focus on a variety of elements that the children may see on the visit or walk, or you could decide beforehand what the focus might be, e.g:

  - geographical landmarks
  - services in the area, e.g. bakery, post office, hairdresser
  - flowers and trees

- Encourage the children to discuss the features they see and, using digital and disposable cameras, to take considered photographs as a record of what they have seen and discovered. At the same time, make a tape recording of any sounds that you hear.

- Back at your setting, help the children to print out the digital photographs on computers and recall the features they have seen. Create an initial display of the 'Environmental photo shoot'.

- Listen to the sounds and match them to the photographs and places.

- Have the films from the disposable cameras developed and use these to remind the children of their outing at a slightly later date as a recall exercise. Add these to the display, following discussion. The children can contribute to the final display by adding their own drawings or paintings of the event, together with emergent writing about the experiences and the various features that they remember.

- When the display is dismantled, keep the photographs and the children's work in a photograph album and add it to the children's library or book corner to encourage them to reflect on the experiences at their leisure.

> " On visits outside the classroom - wonderful adventures can take place. "
>
> *Bronwen Hughes - Teaching and Learning Assistant*

Express delivery

- Set up a transport route with landmarks such as a bus stop, garage, car park and shop around the outdoor classroom. From a central point such as a post office or sorting office, have a variety of letters or parcels ready to be delivered.

- Following a simple route map or spoken instruction (e.g. *Turn right at the garage, straight on past the bus stop*, etc.), encourage the children, either on foot or using a wheeled vehicle, to deliver the post to its destination.

- This activity will encourage very early mapping skills and a familiarity with positional language, used for a real purpose.

Food, glorious food

- Set up an outdoor market stall to encourage the children to consider where different foods come from. Link this to using various information sources to find out about food from all over the world. Use the stall for role-play.

Suggestions for resources – stalls

- fruit
- vegetables   } home grown and from other countries
- food boxes and packets

- dough
- clay   } to make own food samples
- papier-mâché

- vegetable boxes and crates
- artificial grass matting } for display
- awnings and labels

Time-lines

- Create a time-line along a wall or fence and change the time-markers to fit the current time element focus, e.g:

  yesterday • today • tomorrow

  morning • afternoon • evening • night

  Spring • Summer • Autumn • Winter

Or, if focusing on growth:

  baby • toddler • nursery • infant • junior • teenager • adult

- Use the markers to encourage the children to sequence their activities for the day, week, year, life, etc. Encourage them to act out experiences that relate to each marker.

" Young children love to collect, explore and play with sticks, stones, leaves etc. and by using their imagination, their senses and their powers of observation, can find out more about the world around them. "

Bronwen Hughes – Teaching and Learning Assistant

Seasonal role-play

- Create role-play clothes and artefact boxes relating to different seasons of the year and different types of weather. Include seasonal activities and stories in each box to encourage role-play relating to the seasons and the weather, e.g:

Spring box

- raincoats and umbrellas for Spring showers
- gardening tools to plant seeds and seedlings
- an Easter egg hunt game
- baby animal soft toys, puppets or masks

Summer box

- sunglasses, sun hats and beachwear
- sand castle games, paddling pool
- tennis or cricket equipment
- picnic artefacts and resources

Autumn box

- dried leaves, brooms, windmills
- tubs, planters and bulbs to plant in preparation for Spring
- wellingtons and boots for splashing in puddles
- collections of seeds, leaves, nuts, etc. to create Autumn collages

Winter box

- warm clothing, scarves, hats, gloves
- clothes and artefacts relating to Christmas and decorating the Christmas tree
- make a shelter
- snowball and target game

- Change the contents of the boxes on a regular basis to stimulate new ideas for play.
- As each season comes around, create a main focus role-play area for a more extended activity, e.g:

Spring:	The Garden Centre / Spring wedding
Summer:	The beach / The park
Autumn:	The farm / In the wood
Winter:	Santa's workshop / Arctic explorers

Sun and shadow, wind, rain and snow

Use opportunities afforded by different types of weather.

- **On a sunny day, investigate shadows.**

    What can the children's shadows do?

    Draw around each other's shadow with chalk.

    Are their shadows different at different times of the day?

    Can they make their shadows disappear?

    Look at other shadows, e.g. buildings, trees.

    Play Shadow statues or Shadow tag.

    Create shadow puppets.

    Paint on walls, the ground and fences with water and watch it evaporate.

- **On a windy day:**

    Make windmills or wind wheels (paper plates with cut edges folded in and pinned to fences, posts, trees, etc.).

    Make flying birds from tubes with feathers or ribbons for tails. Attach them to string and use like kites.

    Make paper aeroplanes.

    Blow bubbles.

    Watch the clouds.

    Make paper streamers.

    Make paper or plastic sails for toy boats in a water tray.

    Make simple parachutes or kites from plastic carrier bags.

- **On a rainy day:**

    Splash in puddles.

    Chalk around puddles and watch any changes when the rain has stopped.

    Add food colouring, glitter or bubbles to puddles and investigate.

    Make a rain gauge from an empty, clear plastic bottle.

    Construct a canal system with sloping guttering and sail toy boats, etc, along it.

    Try various objects in water to see if they float or sink.

    Have raindrop races on window panes.

- **On a snowy day:**

    Catch snowflakes.

    Make marks and patterns in the snow and observe marks made by other creatures such as birds.

    Make pictures in the snow using a washing-up liquid bottle filled with water – and squeeze!

    Make snowballs, snowmen, snow castles, snow buses.

    Feed the birds.

Animal homes

- Make a collection of soft toy animals and discuss their homes and their needs, how to care for them and respect them as living things.
- Ask the children to create and construct a home for each chosen animal using the outdoor space, the construction equipment and other resources available to them, e.g:
  - a small pool for a frog or fish
  - an underground home for a mole
  - a kennel for a dog
  - a cat basket
  - a cave for a bear, etc.
- Focus on the children's ideas, their choices of materials, the appropriateness of the chosen home, the skills of designing, making and constructing used, and their ability to adapt and improve their designs as they work.

Snail and mini-beast hunts

- Create an environment that will attract small creatures and insects. Encourage the children to look for small creatures within the outdoor environment. Get them to record where they found each creature, using their own methods, so they can be returned to the correct habitat.
- Encourage very careful handling of the creatures. Use poly-gloves for health and safety reasons.
- Create small habitats for the creatures on builder's trays, or in boxes or containers for the children to examine. Encourage the children to create areas in the outdoor environment that will attract small creatures, e.g. wood piles, soil patches, shrubs and bushes. Encourage the children to use a variety of information sources to find out more about insects and mini-beasts.

Off to work

(See Be a 'People person' in Chapter 2, *Language, literacy and communication skills*, as a starting point.)

Create scenarios in the outdoor classroom that will encourage the children to explore the 'World of work'. Many occupations rely on working outside and therefore the outdoor classroom is the most appropriate area for this type of role-play. Assemble boxes, bags, baskets of clothes and artefacts related to different jobs so that the children can act out the role of that worker, e.g. farmer, builder, bus driver, fire-fighter, policeman / woman.

Suggestions for resources

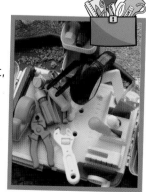

Builder
tool box containing hammer, nails, wood, plasterer's hod, hard hat, tool belt, screwdriver, screws, masking tape, paintbrush, etc.

Fire-fighter
uniform, helmet, hose-pipe, medical kit, small ladder, etc.

6 Creative development

Common teaching and learning elements

- Developing the children's senses in order to respond creatively to their sensory experiences
- Exploring colour, texture, form and space
- Expressing thoughts, feelings and emotions through pictures, paintings and models
- Talking about their work
- Experimenting through role-play
- Investigating and using a variety of media and techniques
- Making choices about colour, media, tools and materials
- Beginning to use their power of observation, their imagination and their experiences to produce creative pieces of work in a variety of media
- Responding expressively and enthusiastically to a variety of music
- Making music by singing, clapping and playing a variety of tuned and untuned instruments
- Participating in singing, rhythm and movement games
- Recognising sound patterns through participating in simple sound, song, rhyme and clapping activities
- Expressing their thoughts and feelings through music, dance and movement

Outdoor classroom opportunities
Seasonal art work

- Base the art work around observation of seasonal changes. Working outdoors gives a different dimension to the way in which children can appreciate art work, e.g:

  - more scope for 'messy' play and art work

  - the opportunity to create something on a grand scale to which all the children can contribute

  - direct observation of nature

  - working in natural rather than artificial light, which gives a new perspective on colour, shade and tone

  - less restriction on noise when using musical instruments

- Encourage the children to base their work on observation of what is around them at different times of the year, e.g:

Spring
- spring flower pictures
- bubble prints
- drip and blow painting

Autumn
- fruit and vegetable prints
- bark rubbing and leaf printing
- Autumn colour collage

Summer
- shadow puppets / pictures
- wet sand modelling
- hand, feet and body prints
- reflective mobiles

Winter
- construct snowscapes
- ice sculptures
- frost pictures (Use a very salty water solution to paint a picture. When dry, it will reveal a sparkly effect.)

- There are numerous art activities using a variety of media and materials that will reflect the changes of the seasons and the accompanying variations in the weather. The vital point to note is that the outdoor classroom will give children much wider scope to create than that offered by the confines of the classroom.

Colour it!

- There is no better place to focus on colour than in the natural light of the outdoors. Focus the children's attention on colours in nature as a natural starting point, e.g:
  - the colours in the sky
  - the different greens and browns in the trees
  - the colours in the landscape
  - 'close-up' colours and those in the distance
  - different shades of each colour

Colour-mixing

- Children will never understand how to create their own colours if they are not first allowed to investigate and experiment with colour-mixing themselves. Powder paint offers a better opportunity for colour-mixing than ready-mix paint as the range of colours will be more extensive and it is also more economical for investigation purposes. Give the children ample opportunity to just explore colour-mixing as an activity in itself before asking them to actually create a picture - **the process is far more important than the end product**.

- Doing this activity outdoors will allow the children to observe colours in nature, work in natural light and be messy without the constrictions that may hamper them in the indoor classroom. Use builder's trays, paper plates, washing-up bowls, and containers of various sizes in which to mix the colours. Encourage the children to 'try out' the colours that they mix on large strips of paper so that they can be compared and discussed at the end of the activity.

- Attach the strips of colour-mixed paper to walls, fences, etc. to facilitate observation and discussion. Use a variety of different-sized brushes to mix and test the colours.

- Once the children are aware that they are able to create colours and shades of colour, opportunities for using colour in a wide range of outdoor activities will develop naturally.

The big and the small

- Often, it is the adult that dictates the size and scale of art work produced by children by pre-determining the size of the surface offered to them, e.g. a pre-determined A4- or A3-size piece of paper.

- If young children are to become experimental artists, they need to be encouraged to make their own decisions about the surface they use. This means the texture, the media (i.e. paper, fabric, clay), the colour, the shape and also the size, e.g:

Big

Use an old white bed sheet. Spread it on a firm, flat surface, e.g. the playground, or attach it to a fence, wall or wooden frame. Encourage the children to create a group landscape by painting onto the sheet with large paintbrushes. Suggestions could be:

- a jungle scene
- the seaside
- in the park
- in the garden

If the scenes are linked to specific role-play activities (as outlined previously), these landscapes, once produced by the children, could become part of the role-play boxes and form various backdrops to the children's play.

Small

Using very small pieces of paper, clay or dough, encourage the children to observe an element of nature very closely with a magnifying glass, e.g. a leaf, an insect, a flower.

Encourage the children, using very fine pencils or brushes and paper, to reproduce the details that they have observed onto the small surface. This concentrates the mind very effectively, and the results can be equally as effective.

When completed, the individual small pieces of work can be displayed as a larger montage.

- Using clay or dough: small slabs or tiles of clay or dough pressed flat can be used as a surface for the children to etch their observations onto or, alternatively, with very small amounts of clay or dough they can be encouraged to produce a model of the observed object.

  The tiles can be grouped together to make a larger mosaic panel of tiles. The models can be displayed in painted landscape boxes (i.e. with an open front and the insides painted as a backdrop), or hung together to make small mobiles.

Feel it!

- Art work can sometimes be limited by the conventional nature of the media and materials that are offered to young children. Art can be created from almost anything. We need, therefore, to encourage children to see the possibilities of using a wide range of materials from the outdoor environment.

Stones and pebbles

Smooth-surfaced stones can be used as a natural surface for small paintings, patterns or designs. Paint mixed with a solution of PVA glue will cling to the surface and, when dry, can be clear-varnished to protect them.

Clay

Clay can be used conventionally to make models or tiles as described on page 45. When mixed with water to create 'slip', a watery solution, it can also be used on a variety of surfaces to create raised surface pictures. If it is put into squeezy bottles, an outline can be 'drawn' by squeezing the slip onto a flat surface and left to dry.

Soil

Using protective or poly-gloves for health and safety reasons (soil contains bacteria), patterns and designs can be etched into a surface layer of soil in containers such as a builder's tray or sand tray using a stick or similar tool.

Sand

- Designs can be 'drawn' into a layer of dry sand in a sand or 'Sahara' tray with a variety of tools.
- Sand pictures can be created using a mixture of sand, paint and PVA glue.
- Create a large beach scene in the outdoor environment by using a sand pit, a paddling pool full of sand, or a large sheet covered in wet sand to have sand castle and sculpture competitions.

Leaves, flowers, wood

- Leaves, flowers and petals can be pressed.
- Leaves and wood can be used for printing and pattern making.
- Collages can be made using natural materials.

Water

- Paint pictures on walls, the ground and fences with a paintbrush and water and watch the design slowly disappear.
- Mix crushed chalk with water and paint pictures and designs onto the playground or a path. These can eventually be washed away with a hose or by the rain.
- Use the chalk and water mix to paint pictures on large pieces of paper pinned to walls or fences.
- Use the chalk and water mix to create play mats and landscapes for small-world toys.
- Mix water with icing sugar to create pictures that crystallise as they dry.

Sing out loud!

- Choose simple songs and rhymes and create play boxes to accompany them, e.g:

Ten Green Bottles

1 Use ten plastic bottles, containing some water to make them sturdier, to act as skittles. Number them.
2 Place them on a low wall or a similar raised surface.
3 Use a beach ball, or similar, to knock the bottles over as the children sing the song.

Five Little Speckled Frogs

The play box could contain five toy frogs, a piece of blue material to form the pond and a pretend (or real) log. The children act out the song as they sing.

Ten in the Bed

The play box could contain a duvet or blanket for the children to lie on and a soft surface such as grass for the children to roll 'out of bed' onto. The children act out the song as they sing.

Polly Put the Kettle On

The play box could contain clothes to dress up as Polly and Suki, a kettle and a tea-set.

She'll be Coming Round the Mountain

The play box could contain all the items that 'she' will be wearing and the artefacts that she will be using, depending on which verses the children have learned or made up. This box could be added to as the children make up extra verses.

Old MacDonald

The play box could contain masks of the animals in the song, the farmer's clothes and hat.

Circle games

- These are a must in the outdoor area. Create a circle game container with picture and / or word cards identifying the circle song, e.g. The Farmer's in His Den, Lucy Locket, Oranges and Lemons. The children choose the appropriate clothing or artefacts from the container in order to act out the circle song.

Sound trails

- Set up a sound trail where the children are given clues to sounds they need to find or make at various points along the trail. Create a sound montage that reflects the sound heard on the trail.

Making sounds

- Make up stories that involve the 'instruments'. The children then act out the stories, using the instruments in the appropriate places.

Suggestions for resources

Shakers:	empty cartons or pots, beads, seeds, buttons, bunches of keys, tubes, washing-up liquid bottles, dried peas, pasta, beans, sugar, sand
Drums:	plastic buckets, waste bins, biscuit tins, plastic bowls, saucepans, washing-up bowls, wooden spoons, pastry brushes (for softer sounds), garden sticks, doweling, pencils
Chimes:	cutlery, keys, metal objects, hollow wooden tubes

Wind chimes

1 Use small metal objects such as forks, spoons, keys, etc. Tie them onto coat hangers or small hoops. Add a longer string in the middle with a bead, cord tag or cork on the end to catch the wind.

2 Tie to a tree, bush, climbing frame, doorway, or experiment with other effective places on which to hang them.

Marching band

- After a lengthy period of time exploring sounds and how they are made, encourage the children to create their own instruments to form a marching band, e.g:

  - pots and pans, and wooden spoons as drums

  - plastic and cardboard containers as shakers

  - tubes and plastic piping for trumpets

or

- Create a 'bandstand' in which the children can create their own music using conventional tuned and untuned instruments, together with those they have created themselves.

7 The role of the adult

Common teaching and learning elements

- Outdoor play will be a valuable, successful and enjoyable experience for children if all the adults working with them are completely supportive towards it.

- Adults need to recognise the possibilities and opportunities that the outdoor environment can offer to young children as learners.

- When outdoor play is seen as a vital part of early years education, it is more likely to be well planned, well organised, well provided for and developmentally appropriate. The role of the adult in the preparation for play, their interaction during play and the assessment of and for learning as a result of play is absolutely crucial.

Before play: Planning and preparation for outdoor play

- The main considerations for organising and managing the outdoor classroom are access, size, design, surfaces, equipment and resources, storage.

- In addition, the role of the adult in planning for that outdoor classroom to be effective as a teaching and learning environment is of utmost importance. Just as we would not expect children to learn and develop effectively in an unplanned indoor classroom, we cannot expect that mere exposure to the outdoor environment will be enough to support effective learning.

- Planning needs to start from where the children are, building on what they know and can already do, and offer challenge, choices and opportunities for decision-making, investigation, problem-solving and discovery.

- In order to plan for children's learning, adults need to assess the learning that has already taken place. The outdoor classroom cannot be seen as separate from the learning that already takes place in the indoor classroom.

- The obvious place to begin, therefore, would be with the experiences that children need in order to develop skills, attitudes, concepts and knowledge (S.A.C.Ks). (These can be found in the common teaching elements which introduce each chapter of this book.)

During play: Active involvement and interaction

- The adult role during play is to facilitate learning rather than direct it. This is done through careful observation, sensitive support, modelling, listening, responding, guiding and extending learning through careful questioning, and active involvement in the play experience.

> " Young children need to see adults being fascinated by nature ... "
>
> *Sheila Meadows -*
> *Head Teacher, Caia Park*
> *Nursery School, Wrexham*

During and after play: Assessment OF and FOR Learning

Assessment OF Learning

During play, the adults will have opportunities to observe and interact with the children to assess what they know and can already do.

They will be able to assess whether the learning experiences provided have given the children opportunities to learn new skills, attitudes and concepts, and gain knowledge.

They will be able to assess whether the children have achieved the learning outcome that the play activity was designed to support.

Assessment FOR Learning

When all this information is assimilated, the adults will then be in a position to evaluate the success of the teaching and learning, and will be able to plan for the next steps in the child's or children's development. This forms the basis of the **Teaching and Learning Plan** that follows.

The Outdoor Classroom – Sample Teaching and Learning Plan

Teaching and learning element	Play opportunity (starting points)	Resources	Adult interaction	Assessment OF learning	Assessment FOR learning (next steps)

Mathematical development (See page 22.)
• Developing the following abilities in a variety of contexts:
- to classify / sort
- to match
- to order
- to sequence
- to count
	Washing Day (See page 26.)
	• Create a laundry area with a washing line, washing baskets, an assortment of clothes, pegs, washing bowls, water, washing powder, etc.
	• Utilise this area to encourage children to focus on the following as they wash and hang out their washing:
	- capacity
	- sorting
	- matching
	- sequencing
	- colour
	- pattern
	- size
	- shape
		Suggestions for resources (See page 26.)
		• A washing-up bowl or water tray, etc.
		• Water and detergent (be careful to consider the children's allergies, and possibly provide protective gloves)
		• Scrubbing brushes
		• A washing line, pegs
		• A washing basket
		• An assortment of clothes or items to wash, e.g. a variety of socks
		• A play iron and ironing board
		• A table for folding washing onto
		• Containers to sort clothes and items
			(See pages 50–52.)
			Before
			• Ensure that all the resources and materials that you need are available for the activity.
			• Clearly, the best adult interaction is of a spontaneous nature – reacting and responding to the child's actions and conversation. However, there also needs to be a learning focus that will offer you an opportunity to help the child developmentally.
			• Decide upon a learning focus, e.g:
			- sorting socks into large / small sets
			- matching pairs of socks by colour and by pattern
			During
			• Remembering that the adult role is to facilitate learning rather than direct it:
			- observe carefully whilst the child / children play
			- respond appropriately to their actions and conversation
			- ask appropriate questions
			- listen carefully to what the children say
			- interact sensitively
			- model the actions that will lead to the focused learning, e.g. begin to sort large / small socks or match pairs.
			- observe how children accomplish the task:
			  do some find it easy / difficult?
			  how involved are they?
			  what is the level of concentration, perseverance, etc.?
			After
			• From your observations, what would you plan as the next steps for the child / children in order for them to progress developmentally?
				For example:
				i) some children may find the sorting activity easy – some difficult
				
				ii) some children may find the matching of pairs easy – some difficult
				
				iii) some children may not have the language to help them sort / match
				
				iv) some children may not have the recognition of colour / colour names to help them with the activity
				
				v) some children may have found it difficult to concentrate or stick at the task
				
				vi) some children may have found the instructions difficult
				
				The assessment OF learning will dictate the assessment FOR learning.
					For example:
					i) ensure that the children have a variety of experiences of sorting, but with a degree more difficulty in order to challenge their problem-solving skills – create more opportunities for sorting games at a similar level
					
					ii) as above for matching
					
					iii) make a note of the language difficulties the children may have – create further opportunities to use / model that language
					
					iv) focus on games involving colour recognition – create more opportunities for the children to practise their skills
					
					v) the activity may have been too complicated, too long or inappropriate for the moment – create more opportunities for the children to practice for shorter periods, then build up
					
					vi) consider how you worded the instructions or questions and create an opportunity for a similar game using different vocabulary or phrasing, or do more modelling.

The Outdoor Classroom – Teaching and Learning Plan

Teaching and learning element	Play opportunity (starting points)	Resources	Adult interaction	Assessment OF learning	Assessment FOR learning (next steps)

The Outdoor Classroom

Teaching and learning element

Play opportunity (starting points)

Resources

Adult interaction

Assessment OF learning

Assessment FOR learning (next steps)

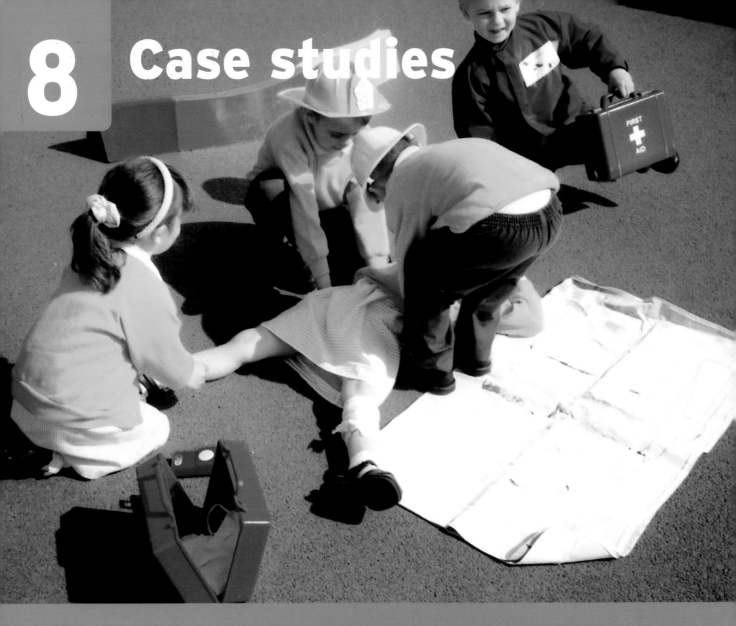

8 Case studies

In researching this book, it was vital to trial the suggested activities with the children to evaluate their effectiveness. This chapter highlights three of these activities, and shows the responses of the children to the learning situations.

Case study 1
Knowledge and Understanding of the World

The Emergency

Learning outcome

- to be able to identify key workers in the Health profession, and be aware of some of their roles

Activity

The children had to respond to an emergency. The scenario was created outdoors following a talk about health services and linked to the Health Centre role-play area indoors. They had read books describing the roles of various emergency services. Then, the children had to decide on the type of emergency, e.g. one group decided a machine had fallen on the victim, having seen a similar incident described in a book. Another group chose a road accident. Others chose a fall from playground equipment, someone unconscious, and someone burnt by chip pan oil, etc.

Possible roles

- 2 paramedics – waiting in the ambulance for a call out
- doctors / nurses to prepare a bed at the hospital
- police to control traffic
- the fire services – to extinguish fires, cut off a car roof, lift machinery, etc.
- a friend to phone the emergency services
- a victim / patient
- controllers for the emergency services to take calls

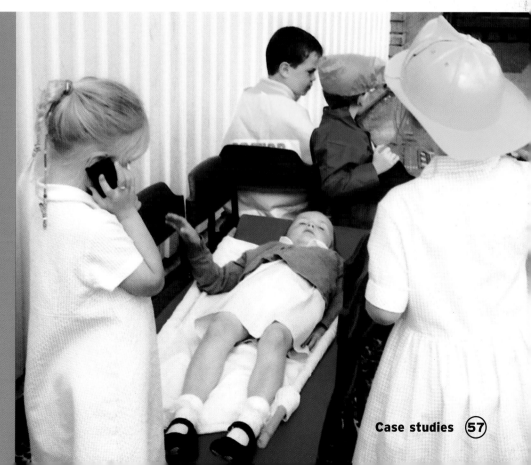

Resources

- 8 classroom chairs to make an ambulance
- fireman helmets, police helmets
- nurse uniforms, police tabards
- unwanted or toy mobile phones
- a stretcher made from plain material, with two poles threaded at the sides (use poles from an old windbreak)
- roll up mats to use as temporary hospital beds
- cheap emergency bleepers (we got ours from the local pound shop)
- toy First Aid kits containing disposable gloves, bandages, plastic syringes, a blood pressure gauge, a stethoscope (the children will soon let you know what they need for the job!)

Questions to ask

- *What number are you going to dial in an emergency?*
- *Hello, which service do you require, Police, Fire, Ambulance, Coastguard?*
- *How many people are injured?*
- *Is there anyone trapped?*
- *Will you require any other service?*
- *Can you describe your location? Where are you?*

Evaluation of the activity

"Superb fun! Wonderful interaction between the children and understanding the need to wait - a huge effort for some as they were so excited - while they waited to be alerted by the switchboard operator. Also, a lot of knowledge can be gained through careful questioning. One group could not decide the number to call in an emergency, 3590, 32710, and one child volunteered 666 - a hotline to the devil!"

Children with limited language could be drawn in through careful questioning, and encouraged to elaborate, e.g:

Where are you?
Here.
Where is here?
There.
What are you near?
The fence.
Is the fence near a shop, or a park or a school?
School.
What's the name of the school?
Borras.
Borras Park Infant School?
Yes.
Good, we will get an ambulance to you right away. Keep your friend talking.

The adult leads the play initially, but the children decide which way it is going to develop. The paramedics, assisted by the police, have to get the patient into the ambulance. This is when one group decided they needed a stretcher. A stretcher was hastily sewn for the next day's play. The children then have to get the patient onto the stretcher and into the ambulance. This usually involves the patient being rolled in an undignified way onto the stretcher, then the children have to load the patient into the ambulance. Remarks such as *Cor, he's heavy* reinforce mathematical learning as the children make comparisons.

From a safety point of view, the adult needs to ensure the 'patient's' head is safe at all times, and there is no risk of real injury, because the children tire very easily when carrying a stretcher, so the ambulance needs to be nearby. The ambulance must then radio ahead to the hospital to tell them they're on their way. A similar procedure is then repeated at the hospital, and doctors and nurses can help in off-loading the patient from the ambulance and carrying to their bed.

Borras Park Infant School, Wrexham

Conclusion

It was a popular role-play area with at least ten children making a plan to use the area at some time on a daily basis.

The swamp should / could have covered a larger area, however it did mean the children had to negotiate over space, and most managed this on the whole, successfully. The children themselves extended the area as they took the dinosaurs into the adjoining shrub area. This area of learning definitely impacted on the children's play with small-world equipment in the outdoor classroom, concentration was increased, negotiation skills were developed.

Resources

- books: *Harry and the Dinosaurs say Raahh, Romp in the Swamp* and *Play Hide-and-Seek* by Ian Whybrow and Adrian Reynolds (Puffin) *Dinosaur Time* by Michael Foreman (Red Fox)
- round-a-saurus mat – a soft circle of material with a strange head used to sit on and to identify the reading area
- palaeontologist: dinosaur bones were small off-cuts of wood, lollipop sticks, matchsticks (to join them we used elastic bands, pipe cleaners and masking tape)
- green waxed moulding sand available from most early years catalogues
- volcano self-drying clay with a small film canister at the top, baking soda, paint and vinegar

Caia Park Nursery School, Wrexham

Language and literacy

- listen to a good story
- have fun with words and language
- understand some of the functions of writing
- books / stories to include: *Harry and the Bucketful of Dinosaurs* stories
- discover / make up new and strange-sounding words, e.g. names of dinosaurs (*anchieosaurus, round-asaurus, primordial swamp, primeval forest*)
- write labels for our dinosaurs

Personal and social

- take turns, share materials, be aware of others and begin to exercise self-control
- begin to use language of negotiation with peers
- respond positively to new linguistic experiences (the language of the dinosaur world) and enter into conversation with friends using new words (*primordial, palaeontologist*)
- concentrate for lengthening periods of time out of doors, playing with small-world materials, (dinosaurs and the swamp)
- explore and experiment confidently with the materials and equipment found in the swamp area

Dinosaur Swamp

A corner to play out of doors

Knowledge and understanding

- begin to use a variety of information sources, e.g. fiction books, charts, etc.
- begin to experiment with time (long ago, considering the world and what was not in it when dinosaurs roamed the Earth)
- make choices and select materials from a range, exploring their potential (make dinosaur skeletons from wood, tape, pipe cleaners and a selection of materials)
- create a volcano and experiment with substances to make it erupt

Creative

- begin to enjoy role-play and imaginative drama
- discuss work in progress and when completed
- begin to observe and appreciate the work of others
- make a signpost to the swamp
- make dinosaur masks
- assemble dinosaur skeletons
- create swamp scenes and become dinosaurs exploring the garden

Mathematical development

- count, compare, sort and match dinosaurs
- use appropriate mathematical language to describe and classify dinosaurs
- use positional language

Case study 3

Personal and Social Development / Knowledge and Understanding of the World

Forest School

Learning outcomes

- build self-confidence
- care for the environment and living things
- begin to develop an understanding of the world around the children by using the senses
- begin to appreciate the importance of the environment and recognise pattern, shape and changes in the world around them
- develop an appreciation of nature and a sense of awe and wonder

Based on the Danish model of creating schools for young children in a woodland environment, this **Forest School** has been established to provide 3- and 4-year-old children with first-hand outdoor experiences within a woodland setting.

The children, together with Early Years practitioners, parents and Forest School Rangers, follow the trail through the woods to the school and encampment.

Arrival at the Forest School encampment.

" The Forest School Initiative with pre-school-age children has been a wonderful opportunity to watch very young children's sense of awareness about their world being opened up. "

Alice Thomas - Education and Development Manager, Legacy Environmental Education Centre

Time to learn how to make a camp fire with the Forest School Ranger.

The fire begins to burn.

The Ranger is careful to explain the dangers.

Now it is time to toast the marshmallows – keeping a safe distance from the fire!

The children watch as the fire is carefully and completely put out.

The Ranger reads a story about animals and insects that live in the woodland environment.

Everyone looks carefully for woodland creatures as they wander back through the wood.

" Their language and confidence in their abilities has been greatly enhanced by the programme. "

Alice Thomas – Education and Development Manager, Legacy Environmental Education Centre

Time to show what we have found and to talk about our morning's experiences.

This initiative is a collaboration between Wrexham LEA and the Groundworks Environmental Trust at its Environment Centre at Legacy, Wrexham.

Conclusion

There is no doubt that the outdoor environment offers a wealth of exciting, stimulating and enriching opportunities for learning and play.

Learning within four walls is surely an adult concept that has more to do with adult control than with children's well-being. It is, therefore, such a relief, and so refreshing, to see that practitioners are embracing the outdoor environment as a welcome alternative, and much-needed supplement, to the indoor classroom.

This book merely offers a glimpse into the possibilities and potential that await us outdoors in creating a new and more appropriate learning environment for young children.

All we need to do, to convince ourselves of the importance of the outdoors, is to bring to mind our earliest memories of play. Having done this exercise, on numerous occasions with practitioners, during training sessions, the result has always been that 95% of our most enduring memories of play are related to the outdoors.

We owe it to today's children to allow their memories to be as rich, creative, varied and joyous as ours have been.

The hope is that the outdoor classroom is the classroom of the future.

Hilary Harriman - The Author

Hilary Harriman (B. Ed. Hons) has taught in the Primary sector for 26 years – specialising in education for 3- to 8-year-olds, and spending 9 years as the Head Teacher of a rural Primary School.

In 1996, she became a Primary Education Officer, Inspector and Adviser for Wrexham LEA – subsequently taking on the role of Lead Officer for Early Education (3- to 7-year-olds).

Hilary is totally committed to helping children learn through discovery, exploration and investigation. She has created numerous training programmes and packages to support this aim, along with programmes that encourage the use of the outdoor learning environment.

Acknowledgements

My grateful thanks go to the following for their help and support with this book:

Angela Coles

Sheila Meadows, staff, children and parents of
 Caia Park Nursery School, Wrexham

Jane Howells, staff, children and parents of
 Borras Park Infant School, Wrexham

Staff at the Early Years Forest School, Legacy

Staff, children and parents of Ysgol Bodhyfryd County Primary School

Alison and Rachel Heale

Colleagues who kindly provided quotes, and the Wrexham Schools that also trialled the materials and provided photographs:

- Hafod Y Wern Infant School

- Penycau Infant School

- Barker's Lane Primary School

- Hanmer Primary School

Staff and children of Fir Trees Nursery, Stockport

Neil Griffiths and David Rose

My husband, Mike, for his support, patience and encouragement

Photography

Catherine Booth Photography, pages:
1 (middle and bottom), 4, 5, 6 (top), 8, 14 (bottom), 15, 18 (top), 19 (bottom), 20 (middle), 21 (middle), 23 (bottom), 24 (bottom), 27 (bottom), 30, 31, 32 (top), 33 (top), 34, 40 (middle), 41 (middle)

All additional photography courtesy of Wrexham LEA Nursery and Primary Schools.